YOU'RE PART OF A
SCHOOL
COMMUNITY!

BY THERESA EMMINIZER

Gareth Stevens
PUBLISHING

Please visit our website, www.garethstevens.com. For a free color catalog of all our high-quality books, call toll free 1-800-542-2595 or fax 1-877-542-2596.

Cataloging-in-Publication Data

Names: Emminizer, Theresa.
Title: You're part of a school community! / Theresa Emminizer
Description: New York : Gareth Stevens Publishing, 2020. | Series: All our communities | Includes glossary and index.
Identifiers: ISBN 9781538245415 (pbk.) | ISBN 9781538245439 (library bound) | ISBN 9781538245422 (6 pack)
Subjects: LCSH: Schools–Juvenile literature. | Community life–Juvenile literature.
Classification: LCC LB1556.E463 2020 | DDC 371–dc23

Published in 2020 by
Gareth Stevens Publishing
111 East 14th Street, Suite 349
New York, NY 10003

Designer: Sarah Liddell
Editor: Theresa Emminizer

Photo credits: cover, pp. 1, 15 Tyler Olson/Shutterstock.com; background texture used throughout april70/Shutterstock.com; papercut texture used throughout Paladjai/Shutterstock.com; pp. 5, 17 Monkey Business Images/Shutterstock.com; p. 7 ESB Professional/Shutterstock.com; p. 9 Rawpixel.com/Shutterstock.com; p. 11 LightField Studios/Shutterstock.com; p. 13 wavebreakmedia/Shutterstock.com; p. 19 Darrin Henry/Shutterstock.com; p. 21 Sergey Novikov/Shutterstock.com.

Printed in the United States of America

Some of the images in this book illustrate individuals who are models. The depictions do not imply actual situations or events.

CPSIA compliance information: Batch #CW20GS: For further information contact Gareth Stevens, New York, New York at 1-800-542-2595.

CONTENTS

Boldface words appear in the glossary.

What Is a Community?

A community is a group of people living and working together. Each school is its own little community. Where do you go to school? You might take the bus to a public school where you learn with other kids from your neighborhood.

Your School Community

What does your school community look like? You might go to a big school in the city and share your classroom with lots of other kids. You might go to a school where Spanish and English are spoken. Every school is one of a kind.

Who's in Your Community?

You and your classmates are part of the school community. So are teachers, school workers, and the **principal**. Your parents, **coaches**, and bus drivers are community members too! Members of a school community work together to meet shared **goals**.

Community Goals

The school community shares important goals: to keep **students** safe, to help students learn, and to make the school a positive place. Each member of the school community has their own role, or part to play, to accomplish these goals.

Community Roles

Everyone has something to **contribute**. School bus drivers keep students safe on the bus. Crossing guards and safety officers keep students safe at the school. Teachers help students learn to the best of their **abilities**. School nurses and **counselors** help keep students healthy.

Where Do You Fit?

As a student, you play the most important role in your school community. Students have the power to make their school a positive, safe place. The way you behave, or act, each day makes a difference. What can you do to contribute?

Your Responsibilities

A responsibility is something a person is in charge of. As a student, it's your responsibility to come to class ready to learn and work hard. You need supplies, such as pencils and paper. You also need to have your homework done.

Your Behavior

You can make your school community a better place by being respectful. That means treating others as you want to be treated. Try to get along with your teachers and classmates. Listen carefully, wait your turn, and always tell the truth.

You and Your School

By following school rules, respecting others, and being a responsible student, you can help make your school community great. But there are even more ways to show you care. Take part in school **activities** and be a leader for younger students to look up to!

GLOSSARY

ability: the power to do something

activity: something done for work, fun, or other reason

coach: a person who leads a team

contribute: to help a person, group, or cause

counselor: someone who talks with people about their feelings and who gives advice

goal: something important someone wants to do

principal: the person in charge of running a school

student: person who attends, or goes to, a school to learn

FOR MORE INFORMATION

BOOKS

Nagle, Jeanne. *What Is a Community?* New York, NY: Britannica Educational Publishing, 2017.

Peterson, Judy Monroe. *Who Are Community Workers?* New York, NY: Britannica Educational Publishing, 2017.

WEBSITES

Britannica Kids
kids.britannica.com/kids/article/community/626292
Learn more about what it means to be part of a community.

Kids Health
kidshealth.org/en/kids/getting-along-teachers.html?WT.ac=ctg#catpeople
Find out how you can contribute to your school community.

INDEX